Appreciation Motivation: How to Harness the Magical Power of Appreciation

Category: Business & Economics

Copyright Bob Oros-2015

ISBN 978-1-312-25591-3

Author: Bob Oros

Publisher: Bob Oros Publishing

Description: When you show appreciation to others you improve loyalty and trust. People have a basic need to feel appreciated. People need to know you care. If you're the leader, you can raise morale and create loyalty, job satisfaction, and motivation when you express appreciation to your staff for their efforts. You can invest in your employees now and "pay" them with sincere appreciation and achieve even better performance. Or you can "pay" later by seeing your team's performance sink and overall morale decrease. Sincere appreciation will motivate your team to a higher level and achieve more.

Key words: motivation, appreciation, appreciation motivation, how appreciation motivates, motivating your staff, motivating employees.

ISBN 978-1-312-25591-3

APPRECIATION MOTIVATION: HOW TO HARNESS THE MAGICAL POWER OF APPRECIATION

Praise and recognition

As a manager and motivator you can't lose with praise and recognition. The results will always be positive. There's really nothing you can do that's more important or will help your people more than letting them know that you think they have great potential.

People must see you as working to help them. A great leader understands that it's much more important for his or her people to receive recognition than for him to receive it. When your company or your department does something special, give all the praise and all the credit to your people. You will get your share of recognition because you are the leader. But your people may be overlooked unless you point out their contributions. That lets them know that you're working for their success, as well as your own. A great leader will never let his or her people think they are working just to help get a promotion or make big money.

Most people don't expect to succeed. Maybe that's been their history. Maybe they've tried two or three different things and nothing worked out. Maybe they think all companies are going to cheat them and hurt them because they've been cheated and hurt in the past. Many people are so down on themselves and their work that they've decided to expect the worst and save themselves from more disappointment.

When people come to work with you in your business, whether or not they succeed will depend on their expectations of themselves and on your expectations of them.

As a manager, you cannot have expectations of failure. If they expect to succeed they will probably succeed. If your employees expect failure they will probably fail. It's been proven over and over again that things will work out exactly as you see them working out. It's your responsibility as a manager to help employees grow in a positive way. You have to let your people know that you cannot tolerate negative thinking. You must let them know that you know they can win, and you won't accept anything less than their best.

Most people set certain expectations for themselves. These expectations are usually low. They don't have the confidence to set lofty goals, and they're afraid to risk failure.

You can be more objective about your employee's talents and potential than they are. You may be able to set goals for them that are still reachable, yet much higher than they'd ever set for themselves.

Everyone who works for you has talent. You know they can make a contribution or you wouldn't have hired or recruited them in the first place.

Every time you help a member of your staff to set a goal and it's reached, you've helped them build the confidence to reach an even higher goal. If you let people settle for modest goals" you will wind up with average and ordinary people on your team instead of superstars.

How can they be expected to rise to your level of expectation?

No individual will push as hard as he or she will with help and encouragement from another person. Many times, the other person is as responsible for a persons level of achievement as the person himself. People will seldom push to their limit with no one around to watch or encourage them.

Never feel like the goals and expectations of your staff are none of your business. They need a person behind them to help push them forward. They'll never resent the fact that you think they can do great things. Constant encouragement leads to increased expectations.

No one ever gets tired of being told they are great and that you think they can do something really special. You can never encourage your people too much. That applies to new people just starting out and people who have been around for a long time.

Praise, recognition, and encouragement don't produce instant results. It may take months or a year of telling a person how special he or she is before you see any development in their own expectations.

Every time you encourage people or let them know that you believe they can succeed, you build a little bit more of that inner strength. You build a reserve that can be the difference between whether your people quit or stick it out until they win.

You've got to let them know every day that you expect to come out a winner.

Nothing encourages people to work harder and produce quality results like having their accomplishments noticed and praised. Praise and recognition are the most powerful forms of motivation.

Praise and recognition are "the top secret strategies". Until recently this kind of motivation was one of the best-kept secrets in business. It's often ignored in standard management training, but successful leaders have always known its value. People respond better to praise than to punishment.

We all have needs at all ages. We all want to feel good about ourselves and the work we do. We all have the need to feel that we belong to a group, the need to feel appreciated, and the need to feel that e are recognized for our effort.

9

As a manager, it's good business to always be looking for a way to help people fulfill their "inner" needs.

People work for a lot of reasons - to be their own boss, to make money for their families - but one of the main things they want from their job is recognition.

If you start praising for successful behavior, the person will want to get the same kind of recognition again. Everybody wants praise for a job well done. They will be anxious to repeat the actions that gave him such good feelings of recognition and accomplishment.

All through the ages, many people have believed that praise has some sort of miracle-working power. Do you believe in miracles? If not, you may be surprised to learn that many medical doctors and scientists today believe in miracles, even if they cannot understand them. You can praise a weak body into strength, a fearful heart into peace and trust; shattered nerves into poise and power; a failing business into prosperity and success; want and insufficiency into supply and support.

Did you ever notice in the Bible how often praise is associated with miracles?

Animal trainers pet and reward their animals with delicacies for acts of obedience. Children glow with joy and gladness when they are praised. Even vegetation grows better for those who love it.

No one seems to know just how praise and recognition releases energy. But the fact that it does is a common experience. Ever notice how, when someone pays you a sincere compliment, or thanks you for a job well done, your spirits seem to get a shot in the arm?

The lift that you get from praise is not an illusion. Neither is it just your imagination. In some way, unknown to science, actual physical energy is released.

Here is an almost magical way to motivate your staff by literally giving them a self-esteem a shot in the arm.

A nation-wide poll conducted by the National Retail Association asked thousands of workers and managers to list, in order of their importance, the factors that they felt were of most importance to workers. "Credit for work" was the item that the workers themselves overwhelmingly rated number one. The managers rated the same item number seven.

Few of us recognize just how very important it is to an employee to be given credit for the work he has done, to be given recognition and praised for a job well done. When we give them what they are hungry for, they are much more likely to be generous in giving us what we want from them, whether it is their skill, manual work, ideas, cooperation, or what not.

Try it on an employee and watch them immediately "perk up." Also, notice how they automatically become more friendly and cooperative.

It has also been proved that praise actually enables students to make better grades. When students were told just before an examination, "You will have little trouble with this test. It is well within your abilities and intelligence" they made better marks than when their intelligence and ability were run down just prior to the test. Praising their ability increased their ability.

"Bonus systems" that just hand out money to employees, as a "gift" from the boss, invariably fail. But where bonuses and profit sharing are based on merit, and as a means of recognizing a persons worth to the company, production always goes up.

Don't wait until someone does something big or unusual to praise him or her. Be generous with your praise. If your morning cup of coffee is good, tell your wife about it. You'll not only raise her spirits, but the chances are she'll try to brew the coffee even better tomorrow morning.

If your secretary gets out your letter faster than you had expected, tell her so. She'll work even harder to please you.

If someone does you some small favor, show your appreciation and give him or her credit for having done something by saying "Thank you".

Every time you say the words "Thank you," and mean it, you are giving the other person credit - praising him or her for having done something you appreciate. Look for things you can thank people for.

Don't take it for granted that people know you appreciate them - tell them. When you let people know you appreciate what they have done, it makes them want to do still more for you. Say those kind words. Let people know how you feel.

Always have a good word for people every time you see them. Let them know whenever you notice something they've done well.

Always be the person who's saying something good about somebody. Sometimes, you may have to look hard to find something to praise. But it's there, somewhere, because everybody has good qualities.

How do you show appreciation?

Appreciation should be sincere. Say it as if you mean it. Put some feeling and life into it. Don't let it sound routine but special. Those two little words, "Thank you," can be magic words in business if they are used correctly.

Look at the person you are thanking. If he is worth being thanked, he is worth being looked at and noticed.

Thank people by name. Personalize your thanks by naming the person thanked. If there are several people in a group to be thanked, don't just say "thanks, everybody," but name them.

Thank people when they least expect it. A "thank you" is even more powerful when the other person does not expect it, or necessarily feel that he deserves it. Think back to some time when you got a nice "thank you" from someone where it never occurred to you that any "thanks" were in order and you'll see what I mean.

Work at thanking people. Consciously and deliberately begin to look for things to thank other people for. Don't just wait until it occurs to you. Do it deliberately until it becomes a habit. Gratitude does not seem to be a natural trait of human nature. When Jesus healed ten lepers, only one thanked him. But are we very different?

If you still have any doubts that praise and gratitude have miraculous power in them, let me ask you this. If I told you about some man who possessed certain goods and explained that the more he gave away the more he always had left ... would you agree it was a miracle?

Well, that is what happens when you start showing appreciation to other people by praising them and thanking them. The more you give away, the more you yourself have left. Science cannot explain it, psychologists and psychiatrists know it is true.

Start looking for good things in your life you can be truly thankful for. If you want to increase your own peace of mind and personal happiness there is no more certain formula than to start looking for good things in your employees that you can praise.

A number of psychologists got together to see whether they could come up with someone simple rule that would help people lead happier lives, with more peace of mind. They came up with a simple formula which seemed to work miracles. The formula was "Stop Finding Fault."

One of the common denominators of all neurotic, unhappy people is that they are overly critical. They deliberately looked for things to find fault with. Yet when they change their attitude and begin looking for good things in people around them and good things in their circumstances, their own happiness greatly increased.

No one is perfect. And it has been said that there is some good in everyone. Try an experiment. If there is some person who irritates YOU, begin looking for something you can compliment them for. Not only will he or she seem to change for the better; you'll find that your own opinion about them is changing.

Mere flattery is easily seen through and does nothing for either you or the other person. Remember there is always something good that deserves praise if you'll look for it. It is much better to praise a person for some little something - and mean it, than to pick out something big, and be insincere.

It's much better, for example, to say to a woman, "You have the most beautiful hands I've ever seen," and mean every word of it, than to say, "You are the most beautiful woman in the world," if she isn't.

Praise the act rather than the person. Praise a person for what he or she does, not for what he or she is.

When you praise an act your praise is specific and is more sincere. The best results are obtained if the other person knows exactly what they are being praised for. Praising the act rather than the person avoids charges of favoritism or prejudice. It also avoids embarrassment.

Most people feel ill at ease if you say "You're a great person." It makes them feel you are handing them a line.

But if you pick out something specific he or she has done, they feel good about it.

Praise has a tendency to multiply and increase whatever it is aimed at. Praise a person for his work and he will do more work. Praise him for his behavior, and his behavior will improve. But praise him merely as a person and you only increase his egotism and conceit. Many children have been ruined for life by their mother constantly telling them, "You're the most wonderful person in the world." In fact, one reason most of us are so stingy with praise and compliments is the fear that we will give the other person a swelled head.

Praising a person's acts and attributes increase their feeling of self-esteem, which is a far cry from egotism and conceit.

1. Sincere praise miraculously releases energy in the other person, perks him up physically, as well as giving his spirits a lift.

2. The person who is discouraged, doing sloppy work, or just hard to get along with is probably suffering from low self-esteem. Praise can act as a wonder drug to give his self-esteem a healthy shot in the arm, change his behavior for the better.

3. Give others credit for what they do. Show your appreciation of what they have done by saying "thank you.

4. Be generous with kind statements. Gratitude is not a common thing. By being generous with gratitude, you make yourself a stand-out.

5. Increase your own happiness and peace of mind by paying three sincere compliments each day.

The Mary Kay organization has a great program for giving recognition. The foundation of the company is based on the premise that women were not given the amount of praise and recognition they deserved. A system of awards for the various levels was set up and the women who joined the company were motivated to achieve some outstanding results. They were not motivated by the money alone, but by the accomplishment of reaching an objective and being recognized for it. The highest level of achievement in the Mary Kay company is that of a diamond bumblebee. The reason it was chosen was that a bumble bee, because of its size and the small wings, should not be able to fly, however, it goes against nature and does something that is meant to be impossible.

At some of the company award banquets, many of the managers and salespeople would come up on the stage after it was over and get the feel of what it would be like to receive some of the awards, and then go back home working harder than ever to make it happen for them at the next banquet.

A group of third-grade students was used to see what effect praise and recognition would have on their work. The class was divided into two groups and given a math lesson. One of the groups were criticized every time they made a mistake and ignored when they did something right.

The other group was encouraged and praised every time they did something correct and when they made a mistake they were not criticized but encouraged to improve.

After the lesson, they were given the same test to see if there would be a difference. Everyone was amazed when the results showed that the group who received the praise and encouragement did 75% better.

An insurance company had just completed the best year they ever had in their history, nearly doubling their sales for the year.

The new sales manager came up with a slogan for the year; "WE APPRECIATE OUR AGENTS". Then they set up a program to prove it. The entire support staff was told to go out of their way to make sure the sales people out in the field were taken care of and made to feel important. They put together an incentive program that everyone could be a winner, not just a few top producers.

They took it a couple of steps further. At the start of the year, they sent flowers to all the agents wives and said they appreciate the long hours and evenings away from home. During the year they sent monthly cards to their wives showing the great trip they would be going on at the end of the year. The sales that were required to win the trip were very attainable and everyone would be in a position to go. THE PROGRAM WAS SO SUCCESSFUL THEY BROKE EVERY RECORD IN THE INDUSTRY. The person who engineered the program was offered a top position with a competing company and left. The following year they hired in a "run of the mill" manager who did not agree with the program and sales fell dramatically.

Employees are people, each one an important part of your business - not just a cog in a machine that goes through certain motions every day with time out for refueling and maintenance. Your staff has a heart and brains, feelings and ideas - and is made of the same raw materials as you. Their energies are there to be used for their own good and for yours.

The employee needs an answer to this very important personal question: "What is in it for me?" As you put these strategies to use, you will find the job only half begun. This is not a cynical question. It is another way of asking: "How much am I worth?" As owner or manager, you ask yourself the same question? So do your employees. And you must provide answers for them as well as for yourself. What incentives will you give them?

To feel very much a part of the business and to be given an incentive, each employee must understand that he is free to contribute ideas. Management must encourage employee ideas and provide the necessary mechanism for obtaining them. Suggestion boxes and idea-discussion employee meetings are a couple of possibilities. Encourage employees to think about problems of the business. Some excellent ideas for their solution may be forthcoming. As a manager, carefully consider all ideas, and if adopted, commend or reward the giver. If not adopted, a word of explanation and appreciation should always be given.

Successful managers build good attitudes in their employees by keeping them well informed.

Important methods of informing employees include personal communication, use of a bulletin board, regular employee newsletter or newspaper, individual written notices, and meetings.

For example meetings are one of the best forms of management-employee communication. They should be kept short and purposeful. There are two types of meetings, the regular stop meeting and the problem or opportunity meeting.

Staff meetings are usually held for supervisors and department heads. However, all employees should be invited to a staff meeting, probably once a month or perhaps once each quarter. Topics could include coming events, business trends, notable achievements, and employee recognition.

The problem or opportunity meeting is called when someone has a problem or an idea worthy of consideration and assistance by others in the company. After the first meeting, the manager usually sets a period of time for considering the problem or idea. The parties get back together for a follow-up meeting to resolve the matter, having had time to think it over and reach some conclusions. This form of communication and mutual effort contributes importantly to the organization's spirit of teamwork.

These procedures make each person feel important to the success of the business. The employee recognizes his value and sees how his efforts help create success.

Holding regular meetings for the employees is one of the best means of motivating your staff and building self-esteem. The manager can write up the minutes of the meeting and distribute these to all concerned on the same day the meeting was held. This practice summarizes the most important points and makes them readily available for future referral and use.

Managers or supervisors should find time to sit down in private with each employee. Another way to create motivation is the personal conference held in private with each employee. In a friendly manner, discuss both business and personal matters. Such talks smooth out problems and difficulties which may be blocking the motivation of the employee. The talks are also helpful to you, the manager, as you may receive information which would come to you in no other way.

Suppose a particular employee seems to have lost spirit and goes about her job with no enthusiasm. If everything outwardly seems satisfactory, you should carefully consider the action you will take and then invite her to your office for a private talk.

The first step is to discuss her work. Find out why her attitude towards the job is poor. She may feel a lack of acceptance by other staff workers or feel insecure or discriminated against, or there may be other sources of dissatisfaction or trouble. Personal or family problems may be upsetting her. If her problems are business-related, they often stem from feeling "out of things."

In this case, the second step is to get her better acquainted with her working associates, perhaps by involving her in making plans for some special social activity of the workers, appointing her to some committee or asking her to assist the manager in some particular project. This procedure will give Mary a feeling of being someone special, of receiving special privileges which have considerable motivational value. If the problems are of a home or personal nature, perhaps some assistance from a friend of hers or relative could be suggested or arranged to help solve the problem.

The manager is the basic element in a business organization. He or she forms the essential link between the general manager and the employees. The entire organization is dependent on him or her. They must follow the fundamentals of good management- planning, organizing, motivating, and controlling.

Usually, the managers responsible for the training needed within his department. He owes each person under him the opportunity for training and self-improvement and should be entitled to similar opportunities himself.

Increasing the capabilities and productivity of your staff is smart business management. The most important asset of any business is managers and employees. You, as a manager or business owner, are judged not only by the product you sell, the good meal you serve, the restful night's sleep you provide in your motel, or the weekend of fun that your guests enjoyed at your resort. You are also judged by the friendliness of your staff, their alertness, their attitude, how they look, and the way they do their job. What did your staff do to send a satisfied guest or customer on his way or bring him back? Getting people to work for you and with you as a team and keeping them working is never simple. However, these skills pay handsomely in many fields.

Motivators are people who support and encourage their employees, instead of telling them what to do. The best managers are individuals who guide, discuss, and encourage others. With help, employees can achieve outstanding results. A motivator is a colleague and a counselor all rolled into one. Managing a team of individuals is not easy, and certain characteristics make some managers better than others. As with most other business skills, you can learn, practice, and improve the traits of good managers. You can always find room for improvement, and good managers are the first to admit it.

Whether your organization's vision is to become the leading supplier in the world, to increase revenues by 20 percent a year, or simply to get the break room walls painted this year, managers' work with their employees to set goals and deadlines. They then go away and allow their employees to determine how to accomplish the goals.

It's easy for employees - even the best and most experienced - to become discouraged from time to time. When employees are learning new tasks, when a long-term account is lost, or when business is down, you are there - ready to step in and help the members of your team through the worst of it.

The overall performance of the team is the most important concern. You know that no one person can carry an entire team to success - winning takes the combined efforts of all members of a team.

Employees are naturally drawn to things that are pleasing and shy away from things that are punishing. Theories of employee motivation and reward come and go, but the practice of employee motivation still comes down to two basic tactics: punishment and reward. If employees don't do what you want them to do, you punish them with things that they don't desire: warnings, reprimands, demotions, firings, etc. If employees do what you want them to do, you reward them with things that they desire: money, awards, recognition, important titles, etc.

Sometimes you have no choice but to punish, reprimand, or even terminate employees. However, before you resort to that, make every effort to use positive recognition, praise, and rewards to encourage the behaviors you want. As a result, your company will be a much better place to work.

By leading with positive reinforcement, not only can you inspire your employees to do what you want them to do, but you can build happier, more productive employees in the process.

Nothing is as unfair as the equal treatment of unequal performers. Whenever you give everyone the same incentive - whether it's the same salary increase, equal recognition, or even equal amounts of your time - this treatment may initially sound fair, it isn't. Before you set up a system to reward your employees, make sure that you know exactly what behaviors you want to reward and then align the rewards with those behaviors. The key to motivating your employees and getting them to do what you want is to know that what motivates some employees doesn't motivate other employees.

No single prescription can help you motivate all your employees. Each employee has his or her own unique motivators, and your job is to figure out what they are. It is unlikely that your employees are going to walk into your office and tell you what motivates them, you must set the stage to find out exactly what motivates each of your employees.

The simplest way to find out how to motivate your employees is to ask them. Often managers assume that their employees want only money. These same managers are surprised when their employees tell them that other things -such as being recognized for doing a good job, being allowed greater autonomy in decision making, or having a more flexible work schedule - may be much more motivating than cash.

Instead of using threats and intimidation to get things done, create an environment that supports employees and allows creativity.

Employees who are trusted and respected by their managers are much more motivated to perform their best. By including employees in the decision-making process you will improve employee morale, loyalty, and commitment.

Challenge your employees to improve their skills and provide them with the support and training that they need to do so. Concentrate on the positive progress that they make and recognize and reward it whenever possible.

Encourage your employees to speak up, to make suggestions, and to break down the barriers that separate them from one another. Are your employees as comfortable telling you the bad news as they are telling you the good news? The ability of all your employees to communicate openly and honestly with one another is critical to the ultimate success of your organization and has a major role in employee motivation.

Employees are more strongly motivated by the potential to earn rewards than they are by the fear of punishment. A well thought-out and planned reward system is important to creating a motivated, effective staff. Rewards need to reinforce the behavior that leads to the attainment of your companies' goals.

Make sure that short-term goals are attainable and that all employees have a chance to obtain rewards. Even the most successful rewards programs tend to lose their effectiveness over time as employees begin to take them for granted. Keep your program fresh by discontinuing rewards that have lost their power to motivate and bring in new ones from time to time.

Most managers reward the wrong things.

Only 3 percent of base salary separates the average from outstanding employees in American companies.

81 percent of American workers report that they would not receive rewards for increasing their productivity.

60 percent of American managers say that they would not receive increases in their compensation for increasing their performance.

If managers and workers aren't being rewarded for increasing their productivity and performance, what are they being rewarded for?

For an incentive program to have meaningful and lasting effects, it has to focus on performance. Everyone, regardless of how smart, talented, or productive they are, can improve their performance.

In a recent study, 58 percent of employees reported that they seldom received a personal thank-you from their managers for doing a good job even though they ranked such recognition as their most motivating incentive. They ranked a written thank-you for doing a good job as motivating incentive Number 2- 76 percent said that they seldom received these. Perhaps these statistics show why a lack of praise and recognition is one of the leading reasons why people leave their jobs today.

Years of psychological research have clearly shown that positive reinforcement works better than negative_reinforcement. Positive reinforcement: (1) increases the frequency of the desired behavior, and (2) creates good feelings within employees.

Negative reinforcement can create bad feelings with employees. Negative reinforcement may decrease the frequency of undesired behavior but doesn't necessarily result in the expression of desired behavior. Instead of being motivated to do better, employees who receive only criticism from their managers eventually come to avoid their managers whenever possible. And employees who are unhappy with their employers have a much more difficult time doing a good job than do those who are happy with their employers.

Give your employees the benefit of the doubt. Additional training, encouragement, and support should be among your first choices - not reprimands and punishment.

Have high expectations for your employees' abilities. If you believe that your employees can be outstanding, soon they will believe it, too.

Catch your employees doing things right. Although most employees do a good job in most of their work, managers naturally tend to focus on the things that employees do wrong.

Should you reward your employees for their little day-to-day successes, or should you save up rewards for when they accomplish something really major?" The answer to this question lies in the way that most of us get our work done on a daily basis.

Recognition is absolutely critical. You may set a lofty goal for your employees to achieve - one that stretches their abilities and tests their resolve - but remember that praising your employees' progress toward the goal is as important as praising them when they finally reach it.

You may think that money is the ultimate incentive for your employees. After all, who isn't excited when they receive a cash bonus or pay raise? Money is clearly important to your employees. People are very motivated to make enough money to pay for their basic needs. However, after your employees have enough money to pay for these basic needs, additional money becomes less motivating, and other incentives - other than cash incentives - become more important. Most employees consider the money that they receive on the job to be a fair exchange for the labor that they contribute to their organizations. Praise and recognition is a gift, and using it help you get the best effort from each employee.

Incentive programs

To effectively motivate, a definite system of incentives or rewards is also necessary. Such a system requires a combination of several groups of incentives, the most important of which are:

1. Money and recognition.

2. Social prestige.

3. Achievement.

4. Self-esteem

Money. The first thought concerning recognition is usually money. Good pay is vital. However, there are others of major importance-steady work, comfortable working conditions, good working companions, good supervision, the actual nature of the job itself, and opportunities for advancement. Good pay is essential to employee satisfaction and must be carefully considered in all personnel matters. The employee should not feel that he is underpaid. Pay is the best and most tangible form of recognition of the employee's worth to the company.

Besides actual pay increases, other forms of monetary recognition commonly used are a bonus plan, profit-sharing and extra pay for reducing costs (cost reduction programs).

Bonus Plan. When considering a bonus plan, first think about its objectives:

To produce extra efforts from participants.

To favorably direct their efforts.

To provide extra compensation according to the financial success of the company and department. To raise morale and enthusiasm of all the staff.

To increase the profitability of the company.

Any extra reward system should have the following characteristics:

Clearly understood and meaningful to all.

Judged to be equitable.

Be results-oriented and reflect employee performance. High producers should get the big bonus and low producers a low bonus or none.

Be closely linked in time to the performance upon which the bonus is based. A quarterly or semi-annual period works much better than an annual period.

Evaluation should be as objective as possible. Good communication is an essential element in the bonus plan. When formulating the plan, seek free exchange of ideas. The manager must be willing to listen to employees and make constructive changes in the plan when needed.

Suggestions concerning a bonus system:

All employees should be eligible.   If employed in a profit-making department, the bonus should be directly related to the profit of that department. If not in such a department, the bonus formula is determined by the supervisor.

Overhead expenses, over which the employee has no control, should be considered separately when determining departmental profit. Appropriate statements of revenues and expenses chargeable to the department must be prepared according to an accounting method clearly understood and recognized as fair by all.

All persons involved in the bonus should be able to periodically measure themselves during the year. (A financial report of some type should be made available.)

Suggested guidelines:

Must be an employee for 1 year before being eligible for a bonus.

Performance should be objectively rated as being unsatisfactory, satisfactory, or superior, etc. If unsatisfactory, he would not be eligible for a bonus and the manager would explain why to the employee. If satisfactory, the employee would receive the regular bonus, as determined by a formula. If superior, he might receive more, perhaps twice as much.

To determine a bonus for managers, use a variation of the bonus plan. A group of major factors needed for success in a given department is outlined-cleanliness, training ability, service, volume, profit, quality, or cost factors. Assign a point value to these, such as "0" for unsatisfactory "1 " for satisfactory and "2" for superior. At the end of each 6 months, the manager objectively rates the manager on each of the agreed-upon factors. For example, if five factors were being evaluated, a score of 10" would be the best possible. This total is equated to a percentage for the bonus, such as 20 percent of the base salary. If total point score were " 9" the bonus would be 15 percent, etc. Annual salary increases could also be equated to average bonus percentage for the year.

The manager might also be awarded a bonus based on increases in total sales volume. His extra reward could be a percentage of any sales gain plus a percentage of the profit, providing that gross profit amounted to a certain percentage of gross sales. These percentages would be agreed upon by the manager and his supervisors or department heads through mutual discussion and consideration. Thus, subordinates and the manager work out the details of the bonus plan together.

Another possible arrangement is a sliding scale of bonus payments in which increments in sales and profits yield step increases in the percentages of bonus paid.

Profit Sharing. There are two types of profit-sharing plans-the cash plan and the deferred plan. Some companies have both. This is called "combination" profit sharing.

There are several important considerations in formulating a profit-sharing plan.

The employee must be with the company for 1 year before being eligible to participate.

The amount received by each participant should be related as closely as possible to performance. Some may receive more and others less.

41

Under the cash plan, profits to be distributed are paid in cash - usually quarterly, semiannually, or annually. Total profit to be distributed to the employees is usually an amount fixed by a formula. For example, one company's employees receive 33 1/3 percent of net profits before taxes, but not over 15 percent of the payroll.

Under the deferred plan, a trust fund is set up to provide employees with future benefits. The fund is created by contributions from participating employees and from the company, according to a formula. The deferred plan provides retirement, death, supplemental unemployment, health insurance, and disability payments. Also, some plans provide for loan and withdrawal privileges which make possible immediate financial assistance in time of unusual need.

These plans have certain advantages: 1, profit sharing tends to become a unifying force drawing management and employees together, such plans are definitely working 2. incentives, since every employee can see that the profitability of the business and his own personal welfare are necessarily related, and 3. each worker has an incentive to be more creative and think of ways to increase sales and reduce or eliminate expenses.

An alternative to profit sharing, which might be more understandable and appealing to certain groups of employees is cost reduction. Every employee knows that when he breaks a dish, for example, there is a cost to the company. If he knew that he would share in the amount saved by the company by being more careful and efficient, he would have much more interest in helping reduce costs.

Here's how the program works. A certain base period for comparing subsequent periods is established. All expenses in future periods are compared with the base period. Any savings in costs are shared with the employees, usually a certain percentage. The formula used by a steel corporation is a payment of 37 1/2 percent of the savings to the employees. In the service industries, expenses have to be adjusted to the volume of business and inflationary cost increases which occurred during the periods being compared. The relationships can be readily figured and savings determined.

Recognition other than money. Nonmonetary recognition can be tangible or intangible. Examples of tangible recognition: pins or plaques for the length of service or special accomplishments; announcing a promotion with a story and employee's picture in the local newspaper, or advertisement in the local newspaper featuring pictures of key personnel, highlighting their training, experience, and outstanding services.

Intangible means of recognition are less formal. A kind word of praise: "Joe, the gardens, and lawn look just great. We've really got a good grounds' man" builds goodwill and is recognized by both parties as respect and recognition. Or, take employees out to lunch at regular intervals, arrange a party for them, such as at Christmas, or send each one a card on his birthday.

When the "whole person" is involved within an enterprise, the employee is often content with less money than he might make elsewhere, simply because he enjoys his work and experiences self-esteem and accomplishment through his work. It is no longer sufficient to satisfy only subsistence needs. Such a policy is too limited to motivate employees enough for today's competitive business conditions. Superior employee performance will be obtained only when his social and self-esteem needs are supplied on the job. "More money" often becomes an insistent demand when management is concerned only with satisfying minimum cost-of-living needs.

Prestige is built in the relationships between people. Employees, like everyone else, feel a strong need to belong and feel accepted. These are important factors in good employee management. The intelligent and efficient manager carefully considers them when he or she formulates policy governing work incentives for the staff.

Let's consider the social and relaxation needs of your staff. Suppose you encourage a 10-minute rest break. If you provide an attractive room where they can sit down and enjoy a few minutes of each other's company and a little refreshment, important social needs have been fulfilled. Employees become better acquainted and develop friendships. Such a management policy encourages employee cooperation and provides an incentive to work toward the best interests of all of the employees and the business.

Or, encourage social events or special dinners for achieving some goal, an employee's retirement, a special event in the life of the business such as the anniversary of the founding date, or similar occasion. You might plan recreation programs-bowling and softball leagues, swimming, golf, or other group-oriented sport.

Ambition falls off when employees do not have enough to do. The only way to solve this problem is to establish reasonable work production standards for each job. Study and evaluation of standards and worker production should result in a reasonable level of output for each position. Living up to these standards brings a sense of achievement.

Better Placement. Workers will be more productive and interested if they feel they are in the right job, best suited for the occupation in which they are employed, and being used to the fullest capacity. Periodic checks of employee's production and talks with his manager will establish his level of performance. Appropriate adjustments in his job assignment help to keep his work up to his capabilities and are of long-term benefit to both worker and employer.

Some places of business look fine from the outside, and to the customer, but much less attractive behind doors in the work areas. This is detrimental to morale. Also, there are indirect, bad effects on habits and sanitation standards. Working areas should be made light, airy, comfortable, orderly, quiet, and clean. Actual tests have proven that morale and productivity are much higher when employees work in pleasant and clean areas than when the work environment is unattractive and depressing.

Self-achievement tops all other considerations as an additional incentive especially for the more ambitious and resourceful employee. Simply stated, a person knows he or she can climb the business ladder as far as their ability can take them.

This incentive is especially powerful for younger members of an organization. To motivate and keep the services of the most intelligent and capable of your younger employees, you must offer an opportunity for advancement. Openings for positions of greater authority and responsibility occur from time to time, and each business can offer its own particular inducements.

Self-esteem needs differ from others in that it is concerned with the employee's view of himself. Examples are the opportunity for recognition, status in the community, respect, distinction, attention, importance, and appreciation. These are the most difficult needs to provide.

Recognition of achievement is a good example of improving an employee's view of himself. Pins, plaques or recognition in the newspaper are excellent ways to denote worth to the company. Self-improvement, hence self-esteem, can be improved by sending your people to special schools or short courses or paying for home study courses or similar improvement programs.

When you want to praise someone for something he's done right, it's great to tell that person, but even greater if you tell him in front of other people. To the person you're praising, it's even more pleasant, and to the people listening, it's motivation to do what it takes to get praise for themselves.

Public recognition is a strategy to live by in your business. Every meeting and convention should have time set aside for recognizing people who have turned in a great performance. Give people some memento of your recognition, like a plaque or certificate. But remember, it's not the cost or size of the award that counts. It's the recognition. People love being singled out as someone special.

Recognition doesn't have to be an elaborate thing, either. It can be as simple as a hand-written note to say, "You are doing great. I am proud of you," or a phone call to say', "Congratulations." There's something about seeing your name in print that motivates like nothing else.

Never hand out a plaque with only a handshake. Say something special about each award. Spend a few moments talking about the person, his sacrifice and his achievements before presenting the award.

Always recognize 20-25 percent of the people at every meeting. If you have 20 people at a meeting, give five awards. If you have 300 people, give 75 awards.

Put both the husband and wife's name on the plaques. Have the spouse come on stage to accept the award along with the winner. Promote "the team." Have special awards that honor the spouse's contributions, things like "Most Supportive Partner."

People who "slip back a little" deserve recognition, too. Give the "Torn Sweater" award, the "I Almost Made It" award, the "Flash in the Pan" award, and so on. This can be a way of reminding someone who usually does well or has great potential that you know he can do much better. Never give this kind of award unless the person has a fantastic ability and you know he will use the award as a challenge - a positive "kick in the pants."

You can never give too much recognition, as long as it's sincere and from the heart. There is one superstar leader who gives the "Manager of the Day" award!

Start practicing the art of sincere praise and recognition. You will be amazed at what your people can do ... and even more amazed at how much they want to do it!

Enhancing self-esteem with praise and recognition improves feelings of self-confidence, strength, worth, and usefulness to the business organization. Denying this need leads to a feeling of inferiority which brings about discouragement.

Employees who are recognized for their worth to the company and rewarded accordingly will multiply this value by customer satisfaction and profits. These are practical employee management suggestions which will bring about more productive and better-satisfied employees. The team approach and provisions for high-quality supervision are essential elements in motivation. Use of specific incentives (rewards) in monetary and non-monetary forms constitute tangible results for the employee.

Implementing these suggestions in no way implies lack of leadership. In fact, such procedures actually increase leadership ability. Each employee is invited to assist management and is expected to participate in plans and discussions. Thus, management and employees have a similar responsibility in maintaining good leadership. By following these recommendations, the manager can build a better management team and strengthen his position as leader.

Get 100 percent cooperation

The ideal manager today is not a man or woman who has all the ideas. He or she is a person smart enough to use the countless ideas of the employees

Try this the next time you want someone to help you do something.

First, simply ask someone to, "Help me do this." Tell them what they are expected to do. Offer to pay them to help, if you want, but make it plain they are to be paid only to carry out your own ideas. Make a note of the cooperation you get, and the success of your joint efforts.

Next, approach somebody else and ask for help. Only this time don't just ask the other person to help you "do" the job, but also ask him or her to help you "think" about the job. Ask for ideas as well.

Say, "I've got a problem here and I need your help. Here is what I want to accomplish. What do you think about it? Do you have any ideas I could use? What is your opinion of the way I am going about this?"

You will find that you will get some cooperation and help by using the first method, you get 100 percent cooperation and much more actual physical work from the other person, by using the second method.

The reason is simple. By using the second approach you are working in harmony with a basic law of human nature.

It is psychologically impossible for a human being to give you 100 percent unless he or she is also allowed to give you ideas.

This has been proved beyond doubt by records kept on industrial workers. Workers who have no voice whatsoever in management, who cannot make suggestions, who are not allowed to contribute their ideas, simply do not do as much work as workers who are encouraged to make suggestions.

All of us are interested in our own problems more than the other persons problems. When you simply ask someone to do something, his feeling is, "That's your problem." But when you ask for advice and suggestions, you have challenged him - you have in effect given him a problem to solve, and he becomes interested. This principle works at home and it works in running your business.

For example, a tough problem in business is getting people to cut costs. It's a big problem in any business. And one that managers get the least amount of cooperation on.

People support what they help create. When you want to cut costs, don't tell them they have to cut down on any specific item here or there. Instead, tell them it is their problem to work out ideas of their own.

How many wives have you heard complain that their husbands never tell them anything about their business or their plans? Never give them a chance to make suggestions. Yet, you hear husbands say that their wives will not cooperate in saving money, and so on. Many parents believe that their children won't cooperate in something the parent wants doing, yet they never ask the child to participate, but only tell him to "do so and so." They never ask the child to contribute any ideas, only his physical actions.

Marriage counselors have adopted a technique for getting co-operation in the home that is very similar to participative management in industry. It is called "Family Planning Sessions."

The wife, husband, and children get together for a family conference once a week, or once a month. The important thing is that the entire family holds regular meetings during which problems are discussed, common goals are set out, and each member of the family is asked to contribute ideas.

It is amazing what can be accomplished when the entire family participates in managing the family. 'Impossible situations' become ironed out, the family gets along better together, and everyone is happier when each 'Member is not just told to 'do this or that' but is asked to make the problem his own problem and figure out some idea how we can do this or that.

It used to be thought that the job of management was to furnish all the ideas. However, the best management people today realize that the men and women in the plant have ideas, or could have if they were given the incentive to have them.

"What is your opinion?" or "How could we do this better?"

Very often we need the endorsement of another person to get an idea of our own adopted. The best way to get this support is to get the other person to participate in your idea.

Try saying this: "If you were me, how would you go about getting this done?"

How to criticize

Be slow to criticize. When you work with people one-on-one, you can say 99 positive things and one negative thing, and the only thing they will remember is the negative' Your emphasis has got to be positive. You've got to lift their strengths. You must be slow to criticize. I know you are thinking, "Isn't there any action I can take when someone is doing badly? Can I just let it slide?"

The most acceptable form of punishment is lack of praise. This method is much more powerful than criticism. If you withhold praise, you let the person know that he's not one of the leaders. If you're someone who constantly gives praise, hell know he's doing poorly when you stop praising, just as much as he would if you criticized him. You've let him know that he's not on the winning team right now, yet you haven't berated him or said anything negative.

When you feel like criticizing, don't. Spend your time making heroes out of other people. Give the people who are doing the job more attention. Before you know it, the poor performer will be dying to get back into the group that's getting praise and respect, and he will improve his performance to do so. You will accomplish the same end without saying anything hurtful.

When you only single out poor performance, you make people feel bad. They're so down on themselves that they won't do anything. All you accomplish is convincing them that they can't do anything right, so there's no reason to try. And that's not what you wanted at all.

There are times when you must address a problem directly. How can you give constructive criticism without bringing up individual failures? One good way to discuss a "negative" is in a group setting. When several people are present, you can address problems without singling out any individual for criticism. Even though your problem won't apply to all the people in the group, you can get your point across without embarrassing the person who is guilty of the problem. At the same time, you can single out individuals who have handled a situation well, put them in the spotlight, and let everyone see the kind of action that inspires praise and recognition.

When we tell another person, "I'm telling you this for your own good," we're not. We're telling him to bolster up our own ego by pointing out some fault in him.

One of the most common failings in managing people is the way that we (sometimes unconsciously) attempt to increase our own feeling of self-esteem by lowering the self-esteem of another person. Chronic fault-finding, belittling the other person, nagging, are all symptoms of low self-esteem.

However, there are going to be times when the successful manager must point out errors and "correct" those working with him. This is truly an art and one that most would-be leaders fall down on.

Because the art of criticism is so little known the very word criticism leaves a bad taste in our mouths. When we think of the word, we think of those men and women who have criticized badly. We are apt to think of someone "jumping down our throat," "showing us up," humiliating us, beating us down.

The real purpose of criticism is not to beat the other person down, but to build him up. Not to hurt their feelings, but to help them do a job better.

You will never hear a pilot say, "He's always finding fault with my flying. Why can't he say something good for a change". A pilot coming in for a landing is a good example of successful criticism. Frequently, the pilots flying must be criticized or corrected by the tower. If he's off course, the tower doesn't hesitate to tell him so. If he's coming in too low, he's told about it. If he is going to overshoot the field, he is corrected. Yet you will never hear of a pilot getting offended by this criticism.

The person in the tower criticizes the act, not the person. The next time you must get someone back on the track, remember how the airlines "correct" their pilots. Keep in mind that their criticism is not for the purpose of ego satisfaction, but to achieve an end result for both the airline and the pilot. The man in the tower doesn't deal in personalities. His criticism is not blared out over loud-speakers but in strict privacy to the pilot's earphones.

He doesn't say, "Well, if that isn't a dumb way to come in for a landing." He just says, "You're coming in too low."

The pilot isn't asked to do something merely to please the boss. He has a selfish incentive of his own to take the criticism and benefit by it. He is not offended; he actually appreciates it.

All criticism could be given in the same spirit; if it were, equally good results would be achieved.

Strategies for Criticism

1. Criticism must be made in absolute privacy. If you want your criticism to take effect, you must not engage the other person's ego against you. Remember your goal - to achieve some good end result - or get him back on target, not to deflate his ego. Even if your motives are of the highest, and you have the night spirit about criticizing the other person, remember it's how he feels that counts. The mildest form of criticism made in the presence of others is very likely to be resented by the other person. Justified or not, he feels he has lost face before his co-workers or associates.

2. Preface criticism with a kind word or compliment. Kind words, compliments, praise, have the effect of setting the stage in a friendly atmosphere. It serves notice on the other person that you are not attacking his ego, and puts him more at his ease. The natural reaction of a person "called in on the carpet" is to get set to defend his ego. A person with this defensive frame of mind is not receptive to your ideas. By praising a person you bring out the best in them and they will understand you better when criticism is necessary.

How to use praise and compliments to open the other person's mind:

"Bill, that was a swell report you turned in. You certainly covered all the important factors. However, there was one thing. . . ."

"Mary, you have done excellent work ever since you joined our company. We appreciate your efforts along this line. There is one thought for improvement I know YOU would appreciate..."

Jim, you have always co-operated so well in the past. Is there any reason why...

"George, you certainly have been a good neighbor all these years. Do you know. . . ."

"I know from past experience that you are always looking for little ways to constantly improve your work. It occurred to me that. . . ."

3. Make the criticism impersonal. Criticize the act, not the person. Here again, you can sidestep the other person's ego, by criticism of his actions or behavior, not his person. After all, it's his actions that you are interested in any way. By pinpointing your criticism to his acts, you can actually pay him a compliment, and build up his ego at the same time:

"John, I know from past experience that this error is not typical of your usual performance."

"George, the only reason I mention this is that I know you can easily do better. It is not up to your usual high standard."

This way you actually build him up while pointing out his mistakes. Instead of telling him, "You're no good," you say in substance, "I think you're much better than this Performance would indicate."

You let him know you think he is better than the error; that you expect him to do better. This in itself is a powerful incentive to "live up to" your expectation.

RIGHT: "This word is misspelled."

WRONG: "Miss Jones, you are a terrible typist."

RIGHT: "Better check your addition on these figures."

WRONG: "Of all the stupid mistakes."

RIGHT: "You must study harder and bring up this grade."

WRONG: "Why do you have to be so dumb?"

There may arise situations where it would be more diplomatic to point out the thing connected with a person, rather than the act of the person himself. For example:

"Fred, somehow or other the weekly report did not find its way up to the accounting office. (It is Fred's responsibility to send it up.) Do you know what happened to that report, Fred?" This, rather than "Fred, you didn't get the report up to the accounting office in time."

4. Supply the answer. When you tell the other person what he did wrong - also tell him how to do it right. The emphasis should not be on the mistake, but the means and ways to correct the mistake and avoid a repetition or recurrence.

One of the biggest complaints of workers is, "I don't know what is expected of me. Nothing I do seems to please the boss, but yet I am never sure what he wants."

Nothing can lower morale in an office, plant, or home, quite so much as an atmosphere of general dissatisfaction without there being any clear defining of just what is expected. Most people are anxious to "do right" if you tell them what "right" is.

As one worker expressed it, "My boss is always finding fault, criticizing my work. All I know is my way of doing it is wrong. Yet he never tells me what 'right' is. There is no standard to aim at. It's like shooting at a target in the dark, with no idea where the bulls-eye is. All I know is that regardless of the direction I aim, I always seem to miss."

5. Ask for cooperation; don't demand it. Asking always brings more cooperation than demanding. "Will you make these corrections?" arouses much less resentment than, "Do this over, and for Heaven's sake, this time see that you get it right!"

When you demand, you place the other person in the role of slave and yourself in the role of the slave-driver. When you ask, you place him in the role of a member of your team. Team feeling, the feeling of participation, gets much more cooperation than force.

It also makes a great deal of difference whether you put Your criticism on the basis of "I'm the boss, and you'll do it this way because I say so," or whether you put it on the basis of, "Here's what we're shooting for, and here's how you can help achieve that goal."

You'll get much further. if you give the other person a selfish incentive for wanting to change his actions, then if you merely issue an order that he do so.

6. One criticism of an offense. To call attention to a given error one time is justified. Twice is unnecessary. And three times is nagging. Remember your goal in criticism: to get a job done, not to win an ego fight.

When you're tempted to drag up the past, or rehash a mistake that is over and done with, remember the illustration of how the man in the tower criticizes the pilot to bring him in safely. He tells him what he is doing wrong now and once that is corrected and settled, it is forgotten. Neither does the man in the tower "hold it against" the pilot because he once actually made a bad landing.

It is just as silly and ineffective for you to keep dragging up past mistakes and harping on them.

Employers are not the only ones who make this mistake. Husbands and wives drag up mistakes and errors from the past that should be dead and buried. Parents dig up dead issues in dealing with children. This never helps the other person to do better in the present; in fact, it is more likely to have just the opposite effect.

7. Finish in a friendly fashion. Until an issue has been resolved on a friendly note, it really hasn't been finished. Don't leave things hanging in air, to be brought up later. Get it settled. Get it finished. Bury it.

Give the other person a pat on the back at the end of the interview. Let his last memory of the meeting be the pat on the back, instead of a kick in the pants.

RIGHT: "I know I can count on you."

WRONG: "You've been told, don't let it happen again."

RIGHT: "I know you'll get the knack of it-just keep trying."

WRONG: "You've got to show improvement soon-or else."

Remember that criticism, to be successful, must be for the purpose of accomplishing some worthwhile goal for both yourself and the person you're criticizing. Don't criticize just to bolster your own ego. And steer clear of the other person's ego when you must correct him.

Memorize these Seven Strategies and begin to put them into practice:

1. Criticism must be made in absolute privacy.

2. Preface criticism with a kind word or compliment.

3. Criticize the act, not the person.

4. Supply the answer.

5. Ask for cooperation-don't demand it.

6. One criticism to an offense.

7. Finish in a friendly fashion.

The way to win an argument scientifically is just the opposite method that most of us naturally use. Every day some situation arises where we need to persuade another person to accept our own viewpoint. Some point of disagreement comes up with wife, husband, child, boss, neighbor, customer, employee, friend, or enemy. "If only I could get him to see things my way," we say.

Suppose you are a clerk in a retail store and a customer comes in and demands that he be given a new refrigerator for the one he purchased, two months after the guarantee period has expired. You try to explain that the company will repair the old refrigerator - but cannot give a brand new one. The customer cannot see this. How do you settle this difference of opinion?

You are in a conference and your boss comes up with an idea for sales promotion that seems good on the surface. However, you see several serious flaws in the idea, and realize that it may well cost the company too much money and lose more customers than it gains. How do you go about convincing your boss that his idea won't work?

Your wife wants to send your son to a private school. There are many reasons that lead you to believe he will be better off in public school. How do you go about getting these ideas across?

You feel that you deserve a raise and that the company can well afford to pay you more. You mention the idea, and your boss says "We can't afford it now; see me later." What do you say?

The natural thing to do when we run up against a contrary idea or opinion is to argue. It may be only a question of which baseball team is the best - or it may be a question debated by statesmen in the United Nations. Unfortunately, the natural thing is still to attempt to argue down our opponent.

Someone has said that golf is difficult because the golf swing is unnatural. It goes against every natural impulse of how to swing a club. We must learn a scientific, but unnatural swing.

The same thing might be said for the art of persuasion. It is natural to regard someone who opposes our ideas as an opponent to be overcome in one way or another. Yet, what we really want to do is convince the other person, induce him to change his mind rather than to conquer him or beat him down.

When someone opposes our ideas, it is natural for us to take it as a threat and a slap to our own ego. And so it is natural to hit back at his own ego, to become emotional and hostile, to shout, threaten, shame, ridicule, and try to ram our ideas down his throat by intimidation or force. We exaggerate every one of our own so-called reasons or claims and make light of every one of our opponent's points.

But this natural way does not win. Because the only way you can ever really win an argument is to get the other person to change his mind.

The old saying, "Nobody ever won an argument" is true if you mean by argument the shouting session or the ego battle. However, there are ways that you can induce the other person to see things your way.

Even organizations that want to get the general public to change its ideas usually make the same mistakes that you and I make when we are arguing about baseball or politics.

Three Yale psychologists found that the best way to get ideas accepted is to use a low-pressure technique, calmly presenting facts, and leaving out threats or attempts at using force! Low pressure is the secret. In one experiment, an illustrated 15-minute lecture on dental hygiene was given to three different groups of students. The first group got a "strong" appeal, pointing up the dangers of dental neglect: tooth decay, diseased gums, cancer, and the like.

The second group received a "Moderate" appeal, in which the dangers were presented, but in a milder and more factual way.

The third group received a lecture presenting straight information that hardly touched at all on the dangers of neglect.

A week after the talks were given, the students were checked to see which ones had modified their behavior most and were following the practices recommended in the talks. Surprisingly enough, the students who heard the "soft" appeal, with no scare tactics, were more closely following the practices outlined in the lectures than those who had heard the "scare appeal."

Other tests with college students have shown similar results in political arguments. It was found that students were more likely to change their political opinions if the "other side" presented unemotional facts than if they made wild harangues.

Perhaps the most exhaustive research work that has ever been done on arguments was performed by the New York University's Speech Department.

The professors listened to 10,000 actual arguments over a seven-year period. They listened to hassles between taxi-drivers, between husbands and wives. Several business firms cooperated and allowed them to eavesdrop on salesmen and counter clerks. They listened to debates. They made notes of who won the argument, and why.

They came to the interesting conclusion that professional debaters - politicians, U. N. delegates - were less successful than door-to-door salesmen in getting their ideas accepted.

The one big reason turned out to be that the professional debaters seemed to be intent upon beating down the opposition, or "showing up" the opposing argument, whereas the salesman was trying to induce the prospect to want to change his own mind.

They found that the one big mistake most of us make in trying to win an argument is in attacking the ego of the other person.

Tell a man or woman that their ideas are stupid, and they will defend them all the more. Ridicule their position, and they have to defend it to save face. Use threats, or scare tactics, and he or she simply closes their mind against your ideas, regardless of how good they may be.

One of the strongest urges in human nature is self-survival, and this means survival of the ego as well as the body. For our own protection, we have to be careful of the ideas that we accept and act upon. We learn to immunize ourselves against any idea that is seen as an enemy. Friends don't usually come at us hammer-and-tongs, and so to be safe we just close our ears to ideas that come to us dressed up like enemies.

When we attempt to sell ideas, we are really trying to reach the other person's subconscious, because no idea is really accepted and acted upon until the subconscious mind accepts it. "A man convinced against his will is of the same opinion still" describes the man or woman who has accepted an idea with the conscious mind-but, not with the subconscious. Such a person may give lip service to the idea and appear to agree with you, but he is still unconvinced and will not act on the idea.

There is just one way to get an idea accepted by the subconscious mind, psychologists know, and that is by suggestion. Numerous experiments have shown that the harder you try to force an idea into the subconscious - the more resistance that idea meets. It is the old instinct of self-preservation at work again. The technique used by psychologists is to "slip" the idea into the subconscious mind more or less unnoticed.

Ever notice that when someone tells you, "You can't do that," you have an irresistible impulse to do it anyway? Ever notice that when someone tells you "You have got to do so and so," you almost automatically react by saying to yourself, "I'll be darned if I do!"

You will be successful in winning arguments to the degree that you are successful in slipping your ideas past the ego of the other person. His ego is like a guard that stands at the entrance of his subconscious mind. If you wake up his ego or arouse it too much, his ego simply will not let your ideas past This is the all-important point.

Keep it in mind as you study the following strategies:

1. Let him state his case. Don't interrupt. Let him state his case. Remember the magic of listening. It not only wounds the other person's ego to be interrupted and brushed off; we run into what the psychologists call mental set. The person with something on his chest has his mind set all geared for talking. And until he has said his piece, his mindset is not tuned for listening to your ideas. If you want your own ideas to be heard, learn to listen first to the other person.

Ask the other person to repeat his key points is valuable when the other person comes to you hot under the collar. Merely letting him get it off his chest goes a long way to reduce his feeling of hostility. If you can get them to "playback" their complaint two or three times, it drains off virtually all their emotion or steam. This shows the other person that you are interested in his point of view.

2. Pause before you answer. This rule works equally well in a conversation where there is no apparent difference of opinion. When someone asks you a question, look at him and pause slightly before answering. This will let the other person know that you consider what he has said of sufficient importance to "think about it," or "consider it."

A light pause is all that is needed. Pause too long, and you give the impression that you are hemming and hawing, or trying to evade giving a definite answer. If you must disagree with a person, however, the slight pause is important. Come out with a fast "no," and the other person feels that you are not interested enough to take time with his problems.

3. Don't insist on winning 100 percent. Most of us, when we get into an argument, attempt to prove that we are totally and completely right, and the other person is wrong on all points' Skillful persuaders, however, always concede something and find some point of agreement.

If the other person has a point in his favor, acknowledge it. And if you give in on minor and unimportant points, the other person will be much more likely to give in when you come to the big question.

"Yes, I can see you have a good point there but have you considered this. . . ."

"Yes, I can understand why it might appear that way, but...

"Yes, you are certainly right about that all right, but on the other hand..."

79

4. State your case moderately and accurately. The tendency that we have to watch in trying to get our ideas accepted, when they are opposed, is to exaggerate and make too forceful an appeal. Remember that scientifically proved tests show that calmly stated facts are more effective in getting people to change their minds than are threats and force.

One reason we still use the old forceful methods is that they sometimes seem to work. You beat the other person down. You show him up. You get him to the point where "he can't say a thing." Your audience applauds, and you think you have won the argument. But the other person still hasn't accepted your viewpoint, and he will not act upon your ideas.

Benjamin Franklin is generally conceded to have been one of the best idea salesmen of all time. In dealing with foreign nations, he always came out on top, and got what he wanted. He is credited with having put across, against much opposition, the Constitution of the United States.

"The way to convince another," said Franklin, "is to state your case moderately and accurately. Then say that of course you may be mistaken about it; which causes your listener to receive what you have to say, and, like as not, turn about and convince you of it, since you are in doubt. But if you go at him in a tone of arrogance you only make an opponent of him."

The same psychology works-whether you are trying to get an assembly to adopt your views on something as important as signing the Constitution of the United States, or whether you would like your husband or wife to accept your views on how to decorate the house.

5. Speak through the third person. The lawyer who wants to win cases rounds up witnesses who will testify to the points he wants to put over to the jury. He realizes that the argument is more convincing if disinterested third persons say that such-and-such happened, rather than if he says it.

The star salesman uses testimonials of satisfied users. The candidate for public office gets well-known organizations and individuals to endorse him. If he says, "I'm the most honest, most intelligent, and best-qualified candidate in this race," voters may have their doubts. But if a league of upright citizens says the same thing, it is likely to carry a lot of weight.

Applicants for positions carry "recommendations" from third parties that are a lot more convincing to the prospective employer than anything the applicant could say in his own behalf.

Speaking through third persons is especially valuable when you have a difference of opinion and want the other person to see things your way. For one thing, people are naturally skeptical of you when you are saying things to your own advantage. Equally important is the fact that what third persons say is much less likely to arouse the ego of the other person than what you say. Records, statistics, history, a quotation from some well-known person, can all be cited as third persons.

When you ask the boss for a raise it will carry more weight if you say., "I believe my record here will show that I have earned a raise," rather than, "I believe I deserve a raise."

6. Let the other person save face. Many times the other person would gladly change their mind and agree with you, except for one thing. They have already made a definite commitment and cannot change their position in good grace. To agree -with you would be to admit they were wrong. And if he has already made definite strong statements opposing your view, he would almost have to admit that he had lied.

Skillful persuaders know how to leave the door open so that the other person can escape from their previous position without losing face. They leave a loophole that the other person can go through. Otherwise, they may find themselves a prisoner of their own logic. If you would persuade another, you must not only convince him. You must also know how to rescue him from his own argument.

Here are two ways:

Method No. 1. Assume that the other person did not have all the facts to begin with. "Of course, I can well understand how you might have thought so-and-so, since you did not know about such-and-such at the time."

If the other person was wrong, find some excuse for his being wrong.

"Anybody would have thought the same thing under the circumstances."

"I felt the same way about it at first, but then I ran across this information which changes the whole picture."

Method No. 2. Suggest some way that he can pass the buck to some other person. A customer of a department store returns a dress. She took it home and her husband did not like it. "It has never been worn," she says.

The sales clerk examines the dress and sees that it shows definite signs of having been dry-cleaned. Now, the sales clerk can show the customer the evidence and prove she is wrong, but she will never admit it, because she has already gone on record as saying, "It has never been worn." So the smart sales-clerk gives Mrs. Customer a loophole through which she can escape.

The sales clerk says, "Mrs. Customer, I wonder if some member of your family could have sent this dress to the cleaners by mistake. I know the same thing happened to me not long ago - I was out when the cleaning man came and my husband sent a brand new dress out and had it cleaned, along with some other dresses I had in the same closet. I wonder if this could have happened to you - because this dress does show definite signs of having been cleaned."

Mrs. Customer sees the evidence - she knows she is wrong and she has a ready-made excuse for being wrong. There is an open door through which she can escape.

When you have a difference of opinion with someone, your object should not be to "win an argument," but to get the other person to change his own mind and see things your way. You must avoid bringing his ego into play. You must slip "logical reasoning" past his ego, then your clinch it by leaving him a loophole through which he can escape from his previous position.

The following six rules will help you accomplish this:

1. Let him or her state their case.

2. Pause momentarily before you answer.

3. Don't insist on winning 100 percent.

4. State your case moderately and accurately.

5. Speak through third persons.

6. Let the other person save face.

The employee must have good and effective supervision to perform to the best of his or her ability. Poor supervision brings about the opposite results. One-third of all employee job changes can be attributed to poor management. Thus, quality of supervision will largely determine the level of employee performance. Since much personal motivation is derived from a competent supervisor, your efforts as a manager to improve the quality of supervision will reflect directly in higher employee motivation, achievement, and morale.

A successful leader

Only 5% of the population will ever reach their potential for all activities, 95% of the people will never truly be successful. What does it take in our everyday lives to be successful? In order to evaluate this question, it is first necessary to understand what "success" is and what all successful people have in common. It is probably safe to assume that anyone reading this wants to be more successful.

By definition, success is the realization of a worthy goal. Success is different forever individual. For some people, an annual income of $25,000 would be a success, for another, it may be $225,000. Whatever it may be for you, there are specific characteristics that you must have in common with other successful people in order to achieve true success.

Goals are the single most important factor in achieving success. Without a realistic goal, you will never know when you have reached your success level. Successful leaders set goals. The goals must be realistic, measurable and obtainable within the bounds of your own perception. As time passes, your goals can always be adjusted upward to reach your ultimate goal of success. However, if your initial goal is to be worth $1,000,000 by the year end and you are currently only worth $100,000 with an annual income of $50,000 a year and this is November, you most likely will never be able to reach it and therefore, it is unrealistic. Biting off a job in small portions makes the eventual achievement of the total task seem easier and manageable. Successful people constantly set goals, re-evaluate their goals and scale them upward toward even greater accomplishments.

So many people never get anywhere in their lives because they don't know where they are trying to go. If you don't have a destination how are you going to make plans? If you don't know where you're going, how are you ever going to help anyone else reach their destination?

The most successful people are those who set goals early in life. A few years ago there was a study done at Harvard University. The graduating class was polled and it was found that only 3 percent of the class had any clear goals set for their future. Twenty years later, the researchers followed up on that same graduating class. The 3 percent who had clearly defined goals accomplished more and made more money than the other 97 percent combined.

There's nothing mysterious about it. It makes sense that if you don't know what you want to do with your life, or what you want to accomplish, you won't ever establish a working plan of action.

To really move ahead, you need short-term goals and long-term goals. You need to know where you want to be six months from now and two years from now ... even 10 years from now.

There's nothing wrong with making changes in your goals as you go along. It's important to be flexible. The most important thing is to make a conscious choice about what you want to achieve and how you're going to get there.

Wherever you are in your career, stop right now and analyze what you want, what your goals are, and begin a specific plan to reach them. Know what you want, and work toward it every day. Have specific goals, and a specific plan for reaching them.

The six "common denominators," for success.

Have a specific goal

Set a specific time in which to achieve your goal

Develop a plan to achieve your goal;

Decide what kind of price you are willing to pay-,

Write it down; and

Think about reaching your goal every day.

Six simple steps - but there is a power in those steps that have been proven time and time again by great leaders in business.

There are two types of goals, short-term goals, and long-term goals. The long-term goals are the big goals, and they come first. After you've decided on those, it's important to establish a series of short-term goals that will provide you with day-to-day motivation. Set a time frame that gives you enough time to take some serious action, but isn't so far off into the future that you are tempted to postpone the activity.

Short-term goals establish a sense of urgency; they provide you with a deadline in the near future that prompts action.

Anyone can do anything for 90 days. You might set a goal of making 10 sales a week. Make the decision to do whatever it takes to make those 10 sales a week for 90 days. What you might not be able to keep up for two years, you can force yourself to keep up for 90 days.

At the end of that period you've got a great feeling about yourself. You've accomplished something that will pay off financially, and you're ready to celebrate. The special benefit is that, once you've proven to yourself that you can make 10 sales a week, your regular goal of five or six sales will seem like a breeze.

When you set goals for yourself you are setting an example for those people you are managing and motivating.

The magic of 90 days can work for anyone if they really commit to the effort. Encourage your people to set 30-day, 60-day, and 90-day commitments. It's human nature that you need a series of small victories on the way to achieving your big ones. The short-term commitment provides motivation and encouragement to keep pushing ahead.

In order for your goal-setting to be effective, you need some system of reinforcement, some way of rewarding yourself. Short-term goals give you reinforcement. Nothing succeeds like success.

The day you start setting goals, you're a day closer to success.

One of the biggest dangers to achieving your goals - procrastination. We all do it, so nobody thinks too much about it. But continually putting off goal-setting is far more likely to result in failure than any event or incident that will happen to you once you're on your way.

The very best advice on setting goals and making plans is: Do it today. Don't wait until tomorrow or next week. Don't think you're too busy or too tired right now. The longer you put it off, the more settled you will get in your present situation, and the easier it will seem to just drift along where you are right now.

Take the time today to get off by yourself and think about your goals and desires. No matter how old you are, it's not too late to set goals and achieve them. Get serious about your future. When you start seeing your goals turn into realities, you will wish that you had started planning and goal-setting years earlier!

To win, you've got to have ability and the right attitude. You've got to have toughness and determination. But before anything else, you've got to have a dream. Your dream is the glue that holds all the effort together. It's the one thing that, once you have it, no one can ever take away from you.

Our world today is so competitive and so tough that young people starting out sometimes get a lot of hard knocks. One of the saddest things today is that most people have stopped dreaming. Before they've had a chance to develop their potential, they get beaten down by how tough it is. The enthusiasm they once had turns to bitterness, and they decide to just "settle" for whatever hand they are dealt. The older people get, the more and more they forget how to dream; they think that dreaming is only for children, not adults.

To win in life, you've got to be a dreamer. You have got to become excited about your life and your future. The greatest thing about this country is that you can become what you dream about.

What most people really need is to know that there's a chance - an opportunity - for their dreams to come true. Encourage your people to dream. If you want something badly enough, you can still achieve it.

When you approach people to join your company, you can't just sell them a job. People are sick of jobs; they've had other jobs. And many times they've not been good experiences. All they want is a chance. They don't want you to just offer them a job, they want you to offer them a dream and the opportunity to make it come true. If you can offer people a chance to do something special with their lives, a chance to believe in something, a chance to dream again, you have given them the kind of motivation to succeed that they will never have if you just give them a set of duties.

And never underestimate the power of dreaming. Having a dream to strive for just may be the one quality that gives you that "edge" over most ordinary people. We've all heard the expression that someone "has his heart set" on something. All your success and the success of your people are, in the end, built on desire. No matter what the odds are against you, if you've "set your heart" on something, you will have the determination and the motivation to see it through to the end.

Encourage the dreams of your people. Once you've got a dream, you can set goals, build your plans, and act. All great people are dreamers ... some let dreams die, but others nourish and protect them, nurse them through bad days. Goals are not just for business, but for all areas of your life.

If you can see it, you can achieve it. Goals help you see where you're going and how you can get there.

Ask any group of workers, "What is the primary duty of management?" The answer setting goals is likely to be near the top of the list. If setting goals appear near the bottom of the list, you know there's a problem! In most companies, top management sets the overall direction of the organization. Middle managers then get the job of developing goals and plans for achieving the direction set by top management. Managers and employees work together to set goals and develop schedules for attaining them.

To get something done, you have to set a definite vision - a target to aim for and to guide the efforts of you and your company. Goals provide direction. You can then translate this vision into goals that take you where you want to go. With goals, you can focus your efforts and the efforts of your staff on only the activities that move you toward where you're going.

Goals provide milestones to accomplishing your vision. Goals tell you how far you have traveled. If you determine that you must accomplish seven separate goals to reach your final destination and you complete three of them, you know that you have four goals remaining. You know exactly where you stand and how far you have yet to go.

Goals help to make your overall vision attainable. You can't reach your vision in one big step - you need many small steps to get there. Goals enable you to achieve your overall vision by dividing your efforts into smaller pieces that, when accomplished individually, add up to big results.

Once you get into a habit of goal-setting, you will wonder how you ever managed to accomplish anything before. As far as your people are concerned, helping them establish their goals will be one of the most helpful things that you can do for them as a leader.

The best goals are SMART goals. SMART is a shorthand for the five characteristics of well-designed goals.

Specific: Goals must be clear and unambiguous; vagaries and platitudes have no place in goal setting. When goals are specific, they tell employees exactly what is expected, when, and how much. Because the goals are specific, you can easily measure your employees' progress toward their completion.

Measurable: What good is a goal that you can't measure? If your goals are not measurable, you never know whether your employees are making progress toward their successful completion. Not only that, but it's tough for your employees to stay motivated to complete their goals when they have no milestones to indicate their progress.

Attainable: Goals must be realistic and attainable by average employees. The best goals require employees to stretch a bit to achieve them, but they aren't extreme. That is, the goals are neither out of reach nor below standard performance. Goals that are set too high or too low become meaningless, and employees naturally come to ignore them.

Relevant: Goals must be an important tool in the grand scheme of reaching your company's vision and mission. Eighty percent of worker productivity comes from only 20 percent of their activities. You can guess where the other 80 percent of work activity ends up! Relevant goals address the 20 percent of worker activities that has such a great impact on performance and brings your organization closer to its vision.

Time limit: Goals must have starting points, ending points, and fixed duration. Commitment to deadlines helps employees to focus their efforts on completion of the goal on or before the due date. Goals without deadlines or schedules for completion tend to be overtaken by the day-to-day crises that invariably arise in an organization.

By developing SMART goals with your employees, you can avoid these traps while ensuring the progress of your organization and its employees. SMART goals make for smart organizations. Many supervisors and managers neglect to work with their employees to set goals together. The ones that do, goals are often unclear, ambiguous, unrealistic, unrelated to the organization's vision, not measurable, and demotivating.

Although the SMART system of goal setting provides guidelines to help you frame effective goals, you have additional considerations to keep in mind. These considerations help you ensure that the goals, which you and your employees agree to, can be easily understood and acted on by anyone in your organization.

The easier your goals are to understand, the more likely the employees are to work to achieve them. Goals should be no longer than one sentence, and they should be concise, compelling, and easy to read and understand.

Goals that take more than a sentence to describe are actually multiple goals. When you find multiple-goal statements, break them into single, one-sentence goals. Goals should never take more than a page to describe.

Why isn't it always better to have more goals? The greater the number of goals, the less you can focus on any one of them and the less you actually get done. No matter how great a manager or employee you are, you can't focus on everything at once.

 Pick two to three goals to focus on. You can't do everything at once, and you can't expect your employees to either. A few goals are the most you should attempt to conquer at any one time.

 Pick the goals with the greatest relevance. Certain goals take you a lot farther down the road to attaining your vision than do other goals. Because you have only so many hours in your workday, it clearly makes sense to concentrate your efforts on a few goals that have the biggest payoff - rather than on many goals with relatively less payoff.

Review your goals and update them as necessary. Periodically assessing your goals is important to making sure that they are still relevant to the vision you are trying to achieve.

You have many possible ways to communicate goals to your employees, but some are better than others. In every case, you must communicate goals clearly, the receiver must understand the goals, and they must be followed through on.

Communicating your organization's vision is as important as communicating specific goals. Communicate the vision in every way possible, as often as possible, throughout your organization and to significant others such as clients, customers, suppliers, and so forth. And you need to be aware of possible obstacles to this communication: Often an organization's vision is pounded out in a series of grueling management meetings that leave the participants beaten and tired. By the time they reach their final goal of developing a company's vision, the participants are sick of it and ready to go on to the next challenge. When you communicate vision and goals, do it with energy and with a sense of urgency and importance.

As a manager, your primary goal in measuring and monitoring the performance of employees is to help your employees stay on schedule and to find out whether they need additional assistance or resources to do so. Few employees like to admit that they need help getting an assignment done - whatever the reason. Because of their reluctance, it's critical that you systematically check on the progress of your employees and regularly give them feedback on how they are doing.

If you don't monitor it, you won't achieve it. Don't leave achieving your goals to chance; develop systems to monitor progress and ensure that your goals are achieved.

When you quantify a goal in precise numerical terms, your employees have no confusion over how their performance is measured and when their performance is adequate (or less than adequate).

How you measure and monitor the progress of your employees toward completion of their goals depends on the nature of the goals. You can measure some goals, for example, in terms of time, others in terms of units of production, and others in terms of delivery of a particular work product (such as a report or a sales proposal).

The secret to performance measuring and monitoring is the power of positive feedback. When you give positive feedback you encourage the performance of the behavior that you want. However, when you give negative feedback you aren't encouraging the behavior you want; you are only discouraging the behaviors that you don't want.

A positive attitude is the next factor that successful people have in common. Truly successful people have a positive attitude. These people relate to the world on a positive basis. They always look for the "can do" not the "can not do" side of every situation. Successful people truly believe not only in themselves but in the reality of their goals. A positive attitude is contagious and when it is sincere, your employees will relate to you and your activities with a vitality and positive attitude that causes a winning, successful environment.

Research and Development have become extremely important to all major corporations. This is where all new products and ideas evolve. Successful leaders have always understood this principle on a personal level and they constantly strive to improve their own abilities through such methods as formal educational systems, seminars, reading books, listening to ideas the thoughts of others, and in any manner that presents itself to them. Successful people truly believe they can improve themselves and constantly strive to seek methods and means that will help them accomplish this task.

Man's ability over all other creatures on this Earth is the ability to think. Successful people use their talent to improve their lives and control their own destiny. Only you can take the initial step toward the unleashing of the power within your own mind. The power is awesome and at times can be frightening. However, man has abilities of the mind that many people can not or would not believe.

The first step in using your true mental abilities is understanding the triggering mechanisms that is a sure success.

1. Passion - Successful people have a driving force within them that sets them apart from others. A desire, an energy to reach their true potential. This force is a part of them 24 hours a day, seven days a week. It never subsides. Their total existence is sustained for the fulfillment of their goals. The passion within this individual to achieve has been so deeply implanted, that their mental power is driven by this force and will not let them do anything other than achieve.

2. Belief - You will make $100,000 this year if you first believe you can. If you do not believe you can you are telling yourself you want it, but it is truly not obtainable. The truth of life is that man's limits are self-imposed by what the mind is given to believe. If you expand the belief in your own abilities, you will also expand your true realm of accomplishment.

A man of whom all are aware lived his life with adversity, but he constantly believed he could achieve.

Here's record:

Failed in business at age 31

Was defeated in a legislative race at age 32

Failed again in business at age 34

Overcome death of sweetheart at age 35

Had a nervous breakdown at age 36

Lost an election at age 38

Lost a congressional race at age 43

Lost a congressional race at age 46

Lost a congressional race at age 48

Lost a Senatorial race at age 55

Failed to become Vice President at age 56

Lost a Senatorial race at age 58

Was elected President of the United States at age 60

With all the adversity that faced him, President Abraham Lincoln had no reason to continually try. Except for the fact that he believed it was his destiny and measure of success to accomplish this task.

3.   Strategy - A strategy is your game plan of life. The roadmap you will use to accomplish your goals, ambitions and desires. Just to believe you can earn $100,000 a year is not enough, you must design a strategy that gives your life direction and navigates you toward success. The key to strategy is to design a proper strategy to achieve your success without the detours of life, to find the shortest distance between two points.

4.   Clarity of Values - Man must first determine which things in life are most valuable to him. He must determine his feeling about such things as patriotism, pride, love, freedom, excellence, ownership and tolerance. These are values in society, the moral, ethical and fundamental judgements that we, as individuals, deem important. Without a clear system of values for ourselves, it is impossible to believe in something with a passion that has no value to us. Once we have established our individual value system we are then able to determine how we can achieve success based on our priority of values. What must we five up in one hand to accomplish what we desire on the other. Without a value system we can never move forward for we may be trading without increasing our potential for success.

5.   Energy - Without the physical vitality to take action, nothing would ever come of our system to this point. The passion could build, our belief of accomplishment could be overwhelming, we could have the best strategy or map to achieve the ultimate value for our own life, but if not for taking the first step, nothing could ever be accomplished. Great success cannot be separated from physical, spiritual and mental energy that compels us to accomplish the most with what we have to work with.

6.   Bonding Power - We have all known people that have the ability to get along with everyone. The ability to be a chameleon is truly the ability to connect with and bond with others. The ability to build rapport. To effectively communicate, we must realize that we are all different in the way we perceive the world and use this understanding as a guide to our communication with others.

Most managers believe that their employees determine how motivated they choose to be. Managers tend to think that some employees naturally have good attitudes, that others naturally have bad attitudes, and that they (as managers) can't do much to change these attitudes. I'm getting really tired of your negative attitude. Unless you change it, you'll never get anywhere in this company!

As convenient as blaming your employees for their bad attitudes may be, looking in a mirror may be a more honest approach. Studies show that managers have the biggest influence on how motivated their employees are. Do managers recognize their employees for doing a good job? Do they provide a pleasant and supportive working environment? Do they create a sense of joint mission and teamwork in the organization? Do they treat their employees as equals? Do they avoid favoritism? Do they make time to listen when employees need to talk?

For the most part, you determine how motivated your employees are. And when the time comes to recognize your employees, you are the best person to do it - and to reward them fairly and equitably.

When you give out rewards, employees don't want handouts, and they hate favoritism. Don't give recognition when none is warranted. Not only do you cheapen the value of the incentive with the employee who received it, but also you lose credibility in the eyes of your other employees. Credibility with your employees is one of the most important qualities that you can build; if you lose it, you risk losing everything.

59 Appreciation Quotes

Check the ones you would like to implement...

1. A word of encouragement during a failure is worth more than an hour of praise after success.
   Anonymous

2. Any man's life will be filled with constant and unexpected encouragement if he makes up his mind to do his level best each day.
   Booker T. Washington

3. Appreciate everything your associates do for the business. Nothing else can quite substitute for a few well-chosen, well-timed, sincere words of praise. They're absolutely free and worth a fortune.
   Sam Walton

4. Appreciation is a wonderful thing. It makes what is excellent in others belong to us as well.
Voltaire

5. At times our own light goes out and is rekindled by a spark from another person. Each of us has cause to think with deep gratitude of those who have lighted the flame within us.
Albert Schweitzer

6. Correction does much, but encouragement does more. Encouragement after censure is as the sun after a shower.
Johann Wolfgang von Goethe

7. Courtesies of a small and trivial character are the ones which strike deepest in the gratefully and appreciating heart.
Henry Clay

8. Encouraged people achieve the best; dominated people achieve second best; neglected people achieve the least.

   Anonymous

9. Flatter me, and I may not believe you. Criticize me, and I may not like you. Ignore me, and I may not forgive you. Encourage me, and I may not forget you.

   William Arthur

10. Gratitude is not only the greatest of virtues, but the parent of all others.

    Cicero

11. I would rather be able to appreciate things I can not have than to have things I am not able to appreciate.
Elbert Hubbard

12. If the only prayer you ever say in your entire life is thank you, it will be enough.
Meister Eckhardt

13. If you want your children to improve, let them overhear the nice things you say about them to others.
Haim Ginott

14. If you wish your merit to be known, acknowledge that of other people.
Oriental Proverb

15. Let us be grateful to people who make us happy; they are the charming gardeners who make our souls blossom.
    Marcel Proust

16. Never let your head hang down. Never give up and sit down and grieve. Find another way. And don't pray when it rains if you don't pray when the sun shines.
    Leroy "Satchel" Paige

17. No duty is more urgent than that of returning thanks.
    Anonymous

18. Nobody sees a flower - really - it is so small it takes time - we haven't time - and to see takes time, like to have a friend takes time.
Georgia O'Keefe

19. Note how good you feel after you have encouraged someone else. No other argument is necessary to suggest that never miss the opportunity to give encouragement.
George Adams

20. Nothing is more effective than sincere, accurate praise, and nothing is more lame than a cookie-cutter compliment.
Bill Walsh

21. The roots of all goodness lie in the soil of appreciation for goodness.
The Dalai Lama

22. The spirited horse, which will try to win the race of its own accord, will run even faster if encouraged.
Ovid

23. There is a calmness to a life lived in gratitude, a quiet joy.
Ralph H. Blum

24. There is more hunger for love and appreciation in this world than for bread.
Mother Teresa

25. There is no investment you can make which will pay you so well as the effort to scatter sunshine and good cheer through your establishment.
Orison Swett Marden

26. There's nothing greater in the world than when somebody on the team does something good, and everybody gathers around to pat him on the back.
Billy Martin

27. Those who are lifting the world upward and onward are those who encourage more than criticize.
Elizabeth Harrison

28. Treat people as if they were what they ought to be and you help them to become what they are capable of being.
Johann Wolfgang von Goethe

29. Two kinds of gratitude: The sudden kind we feel for what we take; the larger kind we feel for what we give.
Edwin Arlington

30. Until you value yourself you will not value your time. Until you value your time, you will not do anything with it.
M. Scott Peck

31. You need to be aware of what others are doing, applaud their efforts, acknowledge their successes, and encourage them in their pursuits. When we all help one another, everybody wins.
Jim Stovall

32. Nothing is more honorable than a grateful heart.
Seneca

33. One can never pay in gratitude: one can only pay "in kind" somewhere else in life.
Anne Morrow Lindbergh

34. Praise can be your most valuable asset as long as you don't aim it at yourself.
O.A. Battista

35. Pretend that every single person you meet has a sign around his or her neck that says, Make Me Feel Important. Not only will you succeed in sales, you will succeed in life.
Mary Kay Ash

36. Promise yourself to be just as enthusiastic about the success of others as you are about your own.
Christian Larson

37. Reflect upon your present blessings - of which every man has many - not on your past misfortunes, of which all men have some.
Charles Dickens

38. Respect a man, and he will do all the more.
   John Wooden

39. Rough diamonds may sometimes be mistaken for worthless pebbles.
   Sir Thomas Browne

40. Teachers: two kinds: the kind that fill you with so much quail shot that you can't move and the kind that just give you a little prod from behind and you jump to the skies.
   Robert Frost

41. Tell a man he is brave, and you help him to become so.
   Thomas Carlyle

42. "At times our own light goes out and is rekindled by a spark from another person. Each of us has cause to think with deep gratitude of those who have lighted the flame within us."
Albert Schweitzer

43. Go to foreign countries and you will get to know the good things one possesses at home. -
Johann Wolfgang Von Goethe

44. "Life without thankfulness is devoid of love and passion. Hope without thankfulness is lacking in fine perception. Faith without thankfulness lacks strength and fortitude. Every virtue divorced from thankfulness is maimed and limps along the spiritual road."
John Henry Jowett

45. "For each new morning with its light, for rest and shelter of the night, for health and food, for love and friends, for everything Thy goodness sends."
Ralph Waldo Emerson

46. "Silent gratitude isn't much use to anyone."
G.B. Stern

47. "God gave you a gift of 86,400 seconds today. Have you used one to say "thank you?"
William A. Ward

48. "No one is as capable of gratitude as one who has emerged from the kingdom of night."
Elie Wiesel

49. "Gratitude is a vaccine, an antitoxin, and an antiseptic"
John Henry Jowett

50. "Feeling grateful or appreciative of someone or something in your life actually attracts more of the things that you appreciate and value into your life."
Christiane Northrup

51. "Appreciation can make a day, even change a life. Your willingness to put it into words is all that is necessary."
Margaret Cousins

52. "Develop an attitude of gratitude, and give thanks for everything that happens to you, knowing that every step forward is a step toward achieving something bigger and better than your current situation."
Brian Tracy

53. "The hardest arithmetic to master is that which enables us to count our blessings."
Eric Hoffer

54. "Feeling gratitude and not expressing it is like wrapping a present and not giving it."
William Arthur Ward

55. "Let us rise up and be thankful, for if we didn't learn a lot today, at least we learned a little, and if we didn't learn a little, at least we didn't get sick, and if we got sick, at least we didn't die; so, let us all be thankful."
Buddha

56. "To educate yourself for the feeling of gratitude means to take nothing for granted, but to always seek out and value the kind that will stand behind the action. Nothing that is done for you is a matter of course. Everything originates in a will for the good, which is directed at you. Train yourself never to put off the word or action for the expression of gratitude."
Albert Schweitzer

57. "Let's be grateful for those who give us happiness; they are the charming gardeners who make our soul bloom."
Marcel Proust

58. "Saying thank you is more than good manners. It is good spirituality."
Alfred Painter

59. Be anxious for nothing, but in everything by prayer and supplication, with thanksgiving, let your requests be made known to God;
The Bible Phil 4:6 NKJV

www.ingramcontent.com/pod-product-compliance
Lightning Source LLC
Chambersburg PA
CBHW022004170526
45157CB00003B/1137